ITALIAN GREYH

NECK
Long, graceful, and slender

SHOULDER
Long and sloping

TAIL
Slender, long, set low

HINDLEGS
Long, well-muscled

FORELEGS
Long, straight

FEET
Harefoot with well-arched toes.

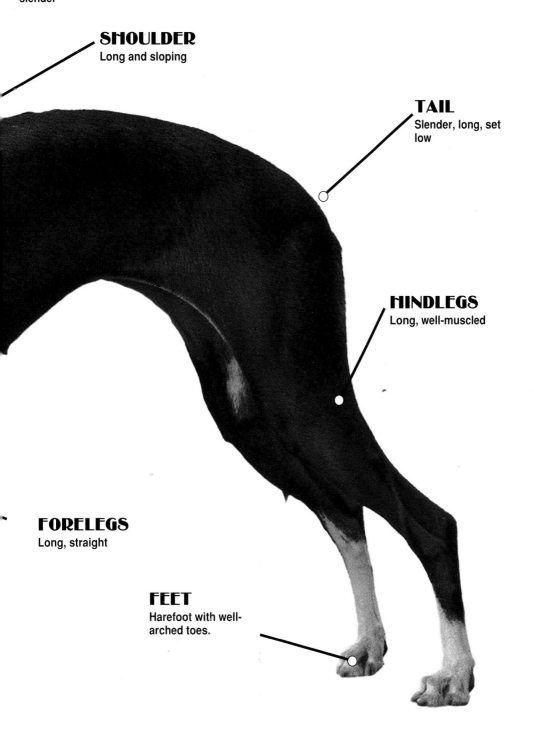

Title Page: Italian Greyhound photographed by Isabelle Francais.

Photographers: Isabelle Francais, Adrien Tudor, Pets by Paulette

© **by T.F.H. Publications, Inc.**

Distributed in the UNITED STATES to the Pet Trade by T.F.H. Publications, Inc., One T.F.H. Plaza, Neptune City, NJ 07753; on the Internet at www.tfh.com; in CANADA Rolf C. Hagen Inc., 3225 Sartelon St. Laurent-Montreal Quebec H4R 1E8; Pet Trade by H & L Pet Supplies Inc., 27 Kingston Crescent, Kitchener, Ontario N2B 2T6; in ENGLAND by T.F.H. Publications, PO Box 74, Havant PO9 5TT; in AUSTRALIA AND THE SOUTH PACIFIC by T.F.H. (Australia), Pty. Ltd., Box 149, Brookvale 2100 N.S.W., Australia; in NEW ZEALAND by Brooklands Aquarium Ltd. 5 McGiven Drive, New Plymouth, RD1 New Zealand; in SOUTH AFRICA, Rolf C. Hagen S.A. (PTY.) LTD. P.O. Box 201199, Durban North 4016, South Africa; in Japan by T.F.H. Publications, Japan—Jiro Tsuda, 10-12-3 Ohjidai, Sakura, Chiba 285, Japan. Published by T.F.H. Publications, Inc.
MANUFACTURED IN THE
UNITED STATES OF AMERICA
BY T.F.H. PUBLICATIONS, INC.

ITALIAN GREYHOUND

A COMPLETE AND RELIABLE HANDBOOK

Dean Keppler

RX-139

CONTENTS

HISTORY AND ORIGIN OF THE ITALIAN GREYHOUND

The Italian Greyhound, with all his charm and elegance, is believed to have originated more than 2,000 years ago. The remains of petite Greyhound skeletons, accumulated throughout the Mediterranean basin, support this belief and the unique ancient breed has even been reported in the tombs of Egypt. The true Italian Greyhound may have actually developed in the countries known today as Greece and Turkey. It wasn't until the 16th century that an influx of the miniature Greyhounds became excessively available in southern Europe. The Italians immediately admired the breed's beauty, small size, and loyalty, but despite popular belief, the Italian Greyhound did

During the 16th century, the Italian Greyhound was admired for his beauty, small stature, and loyalty and quickly became a favored pet among Europe's most prominent figures.

not acquire his name because the breed originated in Italy. The breed's association with Italian art during the Renaissance is how the name developed.

The Italian Greyhound's popularity wasn't limited to just Italy, though. They were frequently portrayed in numerous Renaissance paintings of such artists as Carpaccio, Gerard David, Van der Weyden, Hans Memling, and several others. Early Renaissance paintings and sculptures also portrayed the Italian Greyhound in various hunting scenes, human portraits,

The Italian Greyhound's growth in popularity over the last 25 years has been astounding. The breed is now recognized worldwide.

religious art, and many porcelain statues. Various royal European families showed tremendous admiration for the breed. The Italian Greyhound quickly became a favorite pet among Europe's most prominent and privileged figures, including Frederick the Great of Prussia, Queen Victoria, King Charles VIII, Emperor Maxmillan of Austria, and Catherine the Great of Russia. In the late 1700s, Frederick accumulated more than 30 Italian Greyhounds as his own personal pets. Frederick's great admiration for the Italian Greyhound often had him taking his tiny canine companions along during intense battles and later demanding they be buried by his side upon his death.

According to the American Kennel Club (AKC) Stud

Book, the first Italian Greyhound registration in America was in 1886. At first, the breed's rise to popularity was slow, and registrations in America and England were minimal. Both World War I and World War II have been blamed for the breed's decline and near extinction. The first Italian Greyhound shown in the United States was at Gilmour's Garden in May, 1877. By the mid-1900s, the Italian Greyhound began to make a slow but steady growth in popularity, thus leading to the formation of the Italian Greyhound Club of America in 1954. Fortunately, the last 25 years have seen the breed enjoying its greatest recorded prosperity ever. The Italian Greyhound is now recognized worldwide in many different countries including Austria, France, Germany, Holland, Italy, and Sweden. Today, Italian

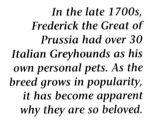

In the late 1700s, Frederick the Great of Prussia had over 30 Italian Greyhounds as his own personal pets. As the breed grows in popularity, it has become apparent why they are so beloved.

Greyhounds are competing successfully in all parts of the world in dog shows, obedience trials, and coursing events, with a growing accumulation of Best in Show awards to their credit. It has become apparent that the admiration of the Italian Greyhound by royal European forefathers was for good reason. It's unfortunate that it has taken the dog world so long to recognize their merit.

Although the popular belief is that the Italian Greyhound was intended only to be a lovable lap dog, he was originally bred to course small vermin. Despite years of domestication, the Italian Greyhound continues to hold on to his excellent sighthound abilities, especially when it comes to tracking and chasing down field mice.

The list of influential foundation dogs and breeders seems endless when it comes to the Italian Greyhound. With that in mind, I will list just a few kennels and top dogs that hold the most influence on the breed today and deeply apologize for those not listed who certainly may deserve to be. Some of the many kennels responsible for the development of the Italian Greyhound breed over the years include Dasa, Flagstone, Giovanni, L'Image, Marchwind, Mira, Rohan, Silver Bluff, Tekoneva, Tudor, and Winsapphire. The influential dogs include Ch. Dasa's King of the Mountain, (top-producing sire of all time), Ch. Flagstone Stock Option, Ch. Dasa's Mountain Man, and Ch. Giovannis Pistacchio. In the show ring, the top winning Italian Greyhound of all time is Ch. Donmar's Scarlet Ribbons.

Although he was intended to be a lap dog, the Italian Greyhound was originally bred to course small vermin. When it comes to tracking and sighthound ability, the Italian Greyhound is superior.

CHARACTERISTICS OF THE ITALIAN GREYHOUND

IS THE ITALIAN GREYHOUND RIGHT FOR YOU?

The Italian Greyhound greatly resembles his larger cousins, the Whippet and Greyhound, and is often compared to the two. Although they share some physical similarities, the Italian Greyhound is much smaller in size and slightly different in conformation. The Italian Greyhound is extremely intelligent, affectionate, long-lived, and very loyal to his owners. It's not uncommon for the Italian Greyhound to become a one-person or one-family dog, forever dedicated to his chosen partner.

Intelligence, affection, and loyalty are some of the Italian Greyhound's most noted characteristics. If you are looking for a lifetime companion, the Italian Greyhound is the perfect dog.

With his sleek form, the Italian Greyhound possesses great agility and speed. It's important to provide your Italian Greyhound with the proper amount of exercise on a regular basis.

The Italian Greyhound is a ball of energy that enjoys the company of other playmates. In a large field or fenced-in yard, they enjoy running and chasing each other, small rodents, squirrels, or even rabbits. Despite their small size, the Italian Greyhound possesses great speed and agility and their coursing abilities should not be underestimated. The quick-learning Italian Greyhound is an eager obedience participant who is always willing to please when training is made enjoyable.

Although small (13 to 17 inches), the Italian Greyhound is a sturdy dog with very few health problems when cared for properly. The Italian Greyhound is not as delicate as he may first appear and therefore should not be babied or pampered. However, small children that play roughly and large, aggressive dogs are probably best isolated from Italian Greyhounds.

Their short, silk-like coat rarely sheds, which makes the Italian Greyhound an ideal pet for those who have dog-hair allergies or don't want the problems associated with caring for long-haired breeds. The Italian Greyhound's petite size makes them excellent dogs for almost every different type of living condition. The Italian Greyhound can easily adjust to an apartment or condominium setting or is perfectly happy wandering on a large farm or field. Although not particularly fond of very cold climates, the Italian Greyhound will adapt quickly if necessary. On bitter cold days, a coat or sweater will suffice in keeping him warm if he needs to be outside for any length of time. For those living in a small city apartment, the Italian Greyhound makes a superb pet, as he can be trained to use a litter box

Opposite: This spotted pair of Italian Greyhounds enjoys a lazy afternoon in the sun.

just like a cat. A few brisk walks during the day will give the Italian Greyhound all the exercise he needs to remain strong and healthy.

Surprisingly, the Italian Greyhound makes an excellent watchdog. Unlike some of the other Toy breeds, the Italian Greyhound has a much deeper bark than one would expect from such a small dog. There isn't a strange sight or sound that will go unnoticed to the keen ear and eye of the Italian Greyhound. In my home, the Italian Greyhounds always bark first to alert me of a stranger passing by or a car in the driveway. The Italian Greyhound is a brave little dog that truly believes he is of tremendous size.

Despite their small size, the Italian Greyhound is a strong and sturdy breed. This agile pup shows off his excellent form and strength.

Italian Greyhounds enjoy the company of other dogs, particularly other Italian Greyhounds. Unlike some other breeds of dogs, a group of Italian Greyhounds easily learn to accept one another from the start. Like other hounds, the Italian Greyhounds will pile on top of each other in pretzel-like fashion when ready for a long night's sleep. These dogs make excellent pets for both the young and old. The Italian Greyhound will respond and interact well with children, provided the child is old enough to understand how the Italian Greyhound must be handled. Al-

Italian Greyhounds have no problems interacting with one another. In fact, like most hounds, they prefer to remain in a group.

though not extremely delicate or breakable, the Italian Greyhound is a Toy breed and cannot withstand vigorous play like some of the other larger breeds. A child must be taught to handle the dog with care and sensitivity. The Italian Greyhound is also appealing to the elderly who prefer a small, compassionate, and loyal dog that is easy to care for.

No matter what the age of the Italian Greyhound fancier, the everlasting charm, energy, love, and clown-like disposition of this breed is what draws so many of us to this fascinating dog.

BREED STANDARD FOR THE ITALIAN GREYHOUND

The AKC-approved standard is the official and ideal description of the adult Italian Greyhound. The objective of any Italian Greyhound fancier, whether owner or breeder, is to own or produce Italian Greyhounds that adhere in structure as close as possible to the standard. Dog show judges use the standard in judging a group of Italian Greyhounds with the ultimate intention of finding which of the participants most closely resembles the standard. The breed standard is important to learn and understand. It is only then that you can recognize what faults your Italian Greyhound may have and how you may correct them if you're intending to take part in an active breeding program.

Although the wide variation of color in Italian Greyhounds is somewhat perplexing, it is acceptable in the show ring. This trio demonstrates some of the different color combinations.

OFFICIAL STANDARD FOR THE ITALIAN GREYHOUND

Description—The Italian Greyhound is very similar to the Greyhound, but much smaller and more slender in all proportions and of ideal elegance and grace.

Head—Narrow and long, tapering to nose, with a slight suggestion of stop.

Skull—Rather long, almost flat.

Muzzle—Long and fine.

Nose—Dark. It may be black or brown or in keeping with the color of the dog. A light or partly pigmented nose is a fault.

Adding to his overall charm and elegance, a long, graceful neck is one of the Italian Greyhound's best features.

Opposite: Italian Greyhounds embody grace and elegance. Their small size is no indication of their confidence and strength.

Teeth—Scissors bite. A badly undershot or overshot mouth is a fault.

Eyes—Dark, bright, intelligent, medium in size. Very light eyes are a fault.

Ears—Small, fine in texture; thrown back and folded except when alerted, then carried folded at right angles to the head. Erect or button ears severely penalized.

Neck—Long, slender and gracefully arched.

Body—Of medium length, short coupled; high at withers, back curved and drooping at hindquarters, the highest point of curve at start of loin, creating a definite tuck-up at flanks.

Shoulders—Long and sloping.

Chest—Deep and narrow.

Forelegs—Long, straight, set well under shoulder; strong pasterns, fine bone.

Hindquarters—Long, well-muscled thigh; hind legs parallel when viewed from behind, hocks well let down, well-bent stifle.

Feet—Harefoot with well-arched toes. Removal of dewclaws optional.

The Italian Greyhound's short coat has a glossy finish and is soft to the touch. Shedding can be kept to a minimum by grooming your Italian Greyhound on a regular basis.

Tail—Slender and tapering to a curved end, long enough to reach the hock; set low, carried low. Ring tail a serious fault, gay tail a fault.

Coat—Skin fine and supple, hair short, glossy like satin and soft to the touch.

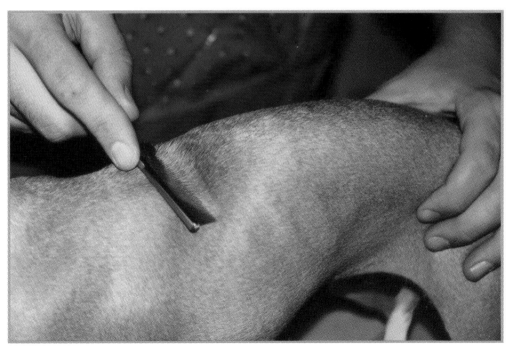

Color—Any color and markings are acceptable except that a dog with brindle markings and a dog with the tan markings normally found on black-and-tan dogs of other breeds must be disqualified.

Action—High stepping and free, front and hind legs to move forward in a straight line.

Size—Height at withers, ideally 13 inches to 15 inches.

For an Italian Greyhound to excel in the show ring, he has to adhere to the official standard for the breed.

DISQUALIFICATIONS

A dog with brindle markings. A dog with the tan markings normally found on black-and-tan dogs of other breeds.

Approved December 14, 1976

INTERPRETATION OF THE STANDARD

It isn't always easy to understand and interpret a breed standard. Some parts of the standard are confusing, contradicting, and misunderstood. For the most part, the Italian Greyhound standard is fairly straightforward and not difficult to understand, but there are some portions that may need further explanation. A part of the Italian Greyhound standard that is often confusing regards the topline of the dog. The standard calls for "high at withers, back curved and drooping at hindquarters, the highest point of curve at start of loin, creating a definite tuck-up at flanks." Several Italian Greyhounds have incorrect toplines— roach or camel back, excessively curved, or dropping off steeply. The best way to understand the difference is to examine a diagram of a correct dog. Even then, Italian Greyhound fanciers will come to realize that standard interpretation differs from breeder to breeder and judge to judge.

Another interesting part of the Italian Greyhound standard is color. One of the great characteristics of this little breed is the wide variation and combination of colors. Italian Greyhounds may be blue, red, red fawn, black, fawn, sable, chestnut, pied, and chocolate with a large number of Irish-marked dogs that have some white on the feet, chest, neck, and tail. Some of the awkward colors are a dilution that has formed from breeding black to other colors, such as the seal, sable, chestnut, and chocolate. The main color variations often leave some breeders scratching their heads in bewilderment from the tremendous varieties and shadings that occur. Although the standard clearly states that all colors are acceptable, with the exception of brindle, serious breeders and show enthusiasts learn through the test of time that there is a partiality that is passed on to judges in the show ring. Unfortunately, a popular Italian Greyhound color will sometimes overshadow the importance of conformation and structure.

SELECTING THE RIGHT ITALIAN GREYHOUND FOR YOU

WHERE TO BUY

The process of finding a healthy and well-balanced Italian Greyhound begins by making contacts with reputable breeders in your area. A good way to start is to consult the ads in dog magazines, at a local veterinarian's, at American Kennel Club (AKC) dog

Make sure you are able to accept the responsibility of dog ownership before selecting a puppy. This Italian Greyhound owner couldn't decide which puppy she loved more, so she picked both.

shows, or by purchasing an Italian Greyhound magazine. The new dog owner must resist the excitement and urge to rush out to a local pet store or the closest breeder for the sake of ease and convenience. Don't purchase a dog without taking the time to thoroughly research the options available in buying the healthiest specimen of the breed. If you have difficulty finding breeders in your area, contact the national breed club, which is always helpful and eager to guide new dog owners in the right direction.

If you acquire puppies from a breeder, be sure to meet the breeder, and see the facilities and the parents of the puppies that they have for sale.

When selecting a breeder, make every effort to learn all that you can about the breeders themselves and the dogs they have for sale. If a breeder is not willing to take the time to show you their dogs and kennel facilities, it may be a clear sign for the buyer to be aware. It is always a positive sign when a breeder volunteers to give you a short tour of his kennel and show you his dogs. If you're calling a breeder from a newspaper ad, be prepared to ask several questions. It's important to inquire about the sire and dam of the litter, the age of the puppies, their sexes, shot records, colors, and most importantly, the price. If the breeder sounds knowledgeable and reliable, make an appointment to see the puppies. Most breeders would be able to explain the different types of dogs on their property from both a pedigree and conformation standpoint. Insist on seeing the sire and dam of the litter if they are on the breeder's premises. The parents of the puppy you purchase should appear healthy, active, friendly, and outgoing. Be certain to ask the breeder what pups or adults they have available, and what they would recommend to best suit your needs. Do you want an Italian Greyhound to show? A dog for obedience? A therapy dog? A lovable pet? You need to answer these questions before making the final decision. Respect the opinions and suggestions of the breeder. Ask as many questions as possible, even if they seem trivial or unimportant. Be prepared to undergo an intense question-and-answer session with the breeder, but don't be insulted.

As a new Italian Greyhound owner, you must remember that a breeder's reputation is on the line and he or she is only concerned about the welfare of the dogs. They have the right to be cautious about who they are selling their dogs to. It's better to work out any quirks between owner and breeder from the very beginning to avoid disasters that may occur down the road.

One way to contact an Italian Greyhound breeder is to attend a dog show. These handlers prepare their dogs for a show.

A dog show is probably the best alternative when trying to contact an Italian Greyhound breeder. Contact local breed clubs or the AKC as to the dates and times of shows within reasonable driving distance. Be prepared to drive at least a couple of hours, but the extra time will be worth it if you can make the necessary contacts. Arrive at the show early, purchase a show catalog, and find out what time the Italian Greyhounds are to be judged. Approach one of the Italian Greyhound exhibitors and kindly ask to speak with them briefly after the judging is complete. Most reputable breeders can be contacted through the show circuit.

PUPPY OR ADULT?

Choosing between a puppy and an adult Italian Greyhound can make all the difference in the world. Before purchasing an Italian Greyhound you must know what to expect from the dog. Are you looking for a top-notch show competitor? An Italian Greyhound to take part in obedience? A therapy dog for a handicapped or elderly individual? A great pet? A combination of all four? The decision becomes a critical one when choosing between an adult and puppy.

If you want an Italian Greyhound only as a pet, the selection of a puppy becomes a lot easier. Once you have chosen a breeder and set up a time and place to view the puppies, the selection process can begin. Before setting up the initial appointment, read as much Italian Greyhound literature that you can. Good places to start are at the local library, in dog magazines, and in breed club pamphlets or articles. If possible, talk to other Italian Greyhound owners about the advantages of puppies as opposed to older dogs. The more information you can get your hands on can only help you better decide between an adult and a pup.

Although Italian Greyhound puppies are irresistible, adults can be just as appealing. Before purchasing an Italian Greyhound puppy, determine what your expectations are for the dog in order to make the right decision.

As a responsible owner, you must devote enough time to training your new puppy. The author and his little Italian Greyhound begin their obedience training with a smile.

There is probably nothing more rewarding for a dog owner than watching your new puppy grow from a lively pup to a fully developed adult. Unfortunately, countless hours of attention, hard work, and many sleepless nights are all factors in a puppy's development. An Italian Greyhound puppy, as opposed to an older dog, will need many lessons in housebreaking and training, as well as constant attention. If you don't have the time to spend on frequent feedings, housebreaking, playing, or anything else an Italian Greyhound youngster requires before reaching the ranks of adulthood, it may be best to choose an older dog. If you have a small child, the choice between a puppy and an adult is an even more critical decision. Small Italian Greyhound pups can easily be injured or traumatized by rough children who are not properly supervised or taught the correct way to hold and handle a puppy. If you have very young children, you will need to take the extra time to explain the difference between holding a toy and holding a delicate puppy. Then, of course, there is always the alternative of acquiring an older dog that may be used to playing with and being around children. In most cases, an older dog is more likely to be housebroken, socialized, leash trained, and safer in the company of a child. I believe that it's best to start with a young puppy so that you can raise and train him the way you wish, as opposed to an older dog that may be stubborn and difficult to break of unpleasant habits. The choice is yours.

MALE OR FEMALE?

Whether you decide to purchase a male or female Italian Greyhound is chiefly a matter of personal preference. There is almost no difference between the two sexes. The only significant difference I've found, which is probably debatable between individual Italian Greyhound breeders, is that the male Italian Greyhound is slightly more difficult to housebreak. Besides that, there is no difference between the two sexes as far as intelligence, friendliness, or personal charm is concerned. From a physical standpoint, the male Italian Greyhound is larger in both height and body, standing an average of 15 inches tall and weighing 10 to 12 pounds. The selection of either a male or female might come down to what may or may not be available in the litter from which you are choosing. If your Italian Greyhound is purchased solely as a pet, you will most likely be required to sign a spay/neuter contract. This enforces the fact that pet animals should not be bred, and that neutering and spaying is necessary. The contract helps to both enforce and discourage the breeding of two pet-quality animals, which is a poor choice from both a health and breeding standpoint.

If you intend to show your new dog, the selection of a male or female may be out of your hands and left up to the breeder. In most circumstances, a female show prospect is more valuable than a male for obvious breeding reasons.

Whether you choose a male or female, a new owner should not be intimidated by the concept of owning a pet-quality animal as opposed to a show dog. A "pet" label on an Italian Greyhound has no bearing on the health, beauty, or overall physical and mental stability of the dog. Italian Greyhound breeders who are solely interested in breeding high-caliber show dogs may classify a dog as a pet for reasons that have nothing to do with the overall quality of the animal. A perfectly bred show dog may become pet quality simply because he has light eyes, is oversized or undersized, is an undesirable color, or has an incorrect ear set. These guidelines are based on the breed standard, which are discussed in detail.

PROPER PUPPY SELECTION

If you are interested in an Italian Greyhound puppy strictly as a pet, then selecting puppies becomes a much easier task. As mentioned earlier, the first step is to contact a reliable breeder through the avenues we previously discussed. For starters, you want a puppy that is friendly, outgoing, full of himself, and most importantly, healthy. Most likely, the Italian Greyhound puppies that you're choosing from will be 8 to 10 weeks old. The most important health factors to consider in your new prospective puppy include shiny coat, bright alert eyes, pink

Because of their fragility, newborn puppies need to be handled carefully. Make sure your Italian Greyhound has all his vaccinations before taking him out to meet people.

Before selecting a show dog, familiarize yourself with the Italian Greyhound standard. A breeder or other Italian Greyhound exhibitor are excellent sources of information.

gums, and adequate weight. The puppy should look strong and thrifty with no discharge from the eyes, ears, or nose. It is best to view the litter of puppies at the breeder's home. This allows you to thoroughly examine the living conditions in which the puppies were raised. Did the litter get plenty of human attention? Perhaps the litter was raised in an isolated spot, such as a basement. Such variables make a difference in the mental and physical health of your new Italian Greyhound puppy and determine how well he will adjust to his new home. A shy puppy that is listless and appears to be backing away from you is a bad sign. A timid puppy is likely to grow up to be a shy adult that will require extra care regarding socialization. If the puppy fits all the health guidelines and appears to have a good disposition, select the one that appeals to you the most. Upon purchase, it is essential that the breeder provides you with a health certificate from the veterinarian indicating that the puppy is in good health overall. The breeder should also supply you with a written account of the puppy's shots, worming, and special feeding guidelines. If the breeder doesn't voluntarily offer this information, make sure you ask for it.

Opposite: Two Italian Greyhounds are better than one. In fact, Italian Greyhounds get along wonderfully together and actually prefer to stay in groups.

SELECTING A SHOW DOG

Before you can successfully select an Italian Greyhound show prospect, you must be thoroughly familiar with the Italian Greyhound standard. This is best understood by speaking with the breeder of the litter or other Italian Greyhound exhibitors who should be able to help you better understand the finer points of show conformation. Because this is your first show puppy, you may not get an extraordinary dog without first proving to the breeder that you are reliable, serious about showing, and willing to put the needed time and money into successfully competing in the show ring. An older puppy will likely cost more for the simple reason that this Italian Greyhound is already at the age where he can be evaluated confidently.

Your Italian Greyhound should be a valued part of your family. Treating him with love and respect will help him to grow into a healthy and obedient adult.

THE ITALIAN GREYHOUND TEMPERAMENT

No matter what type of dog you are interested in purchasing, one of your main objectives should be to find one with a good temperament. The temperament of the Italian Greyhound, like most other breeds, depends on how successful the owner was at socializing the dog from the time he was a small puppy to the point of adulthood. The Italian Greyhound breed has occasionally been criticized for being high strung, busy, nervous, shy, and even spooky. While some Italian Greyhounds do possess these characteristics, it is usually the owner's fault for failing to implement adequate socialization techniques. It's frustrating for me to see a beautiful show dog that will shake, shiver, and back away during an examination at a dog show. There is absolutely no excuse for this type of behavior. Dogs such as these are usually kennel-raised as youngsters, completely deprived of human interaction. Unfortunately, some neglectful breeders will breed dogs that they know have temperament problems.

Proper early socialization is really the only solution to keeping a bad temperament under control. It's important to expose a young Italian Greyhound to as much as possible at a very early age, but be careful not to baby him. If I have a litter of puppies at home, I make sure that every person who visits touches and holds them as frequently as possible. Once the litter is old enough, take them with you on long walks, on car rides, to the flea market, or anywhere else you think they would enjoy. Let the puppies explore everything around them. Italian Greyhounds are sensitive dogs who love human attention. The more people they meet, the better adjusted they will be.

PEDIGREE AND REGISTRATION

A dog's pedigree is simply a family tree that usually traces back his relatives for five generations and includes the dog's date of birth, its sex, sire and dam, and other breeder information. Dogs that are well bred will often have several purebred champion ancestors throughout their pedigree. This becomes more significant when comparing pedigrees of show dogs that are usually carefully bred. AKC registration papers list the sire and dam of your puppy. The breeder you buy from will give you registration papers that enable you to register your puppy. In most cases, the breeder has registered only the litter, and it is the new

Keeping your dog in a crate when you are on the road will prevent him from injuring himself. These show dogs wait patiently for their turn to shine.

owner's responsibility to register his individual pup. The breeder will most likely fill out the sex and color of the dog. You may choose a name for the dog, but in most cases, the breeder requires that his or her registered kennel's name remains as part of the dog's full name.

For most new owners, the acquisition of registration papers, also known as "blue slips," will be contingent upon getting the dog spayed or neutered if you don't plan to show him. Recently, the AKC implemented what is known as limited registration, in which the breeder checks off a box on the registration papers that specifies whether the dog may or may not be shown. Depending on the circumstances, your breeder may provide a contract with specific guide-lines. The papers are then sent out to the appropriate address with a small registration fee charged by the AKC. The AKC will then send the dog's permanent registration back in the form of a white slip that lists the dog's name, date of birth, sex, color, breeder, and new owner.

TIME TO TAKE YOUR
ITALIAN GREYHOUND HOME

To help make your new puppy's arrival as comfort-able as possible, there is some preparation needed. Keep in mind that the first week or so will be rough for both you and the puppy. If you prepare yourself and allow the Italian Greyhound a sufficient amount of time to grow accustomed to his new surroundings, the experience will be much more enjoyable for the both of you. Before bringing the Italian Greyhound home, designate an area in your home where you plan to keep the dog. I would suggest a small, uncarpeted room with a tiled floor because carpet can be soiled and ruined during the housebreaking process. Check with the breeder to see what type of schedule the puppy is comfortable with. How much and what kind of food does the Italian Greyhound eat? Is there a designated time that he eats? How often does he go out? Don't panic if you are unable to keep to a strict schedule. The secret to success is to make all adjust-ments slowly to gradually meet your needs.

The space you choose for the new puppy should be private and confined, which allows him to relax and absorb his surroundings. Feeling secure in his new area is also important. A playpen about four feet in height not only gives the puppy a sense of security, but it also limits his activity. Italian Greyhounds are known to be excellent jumpers for their tiny size. The best investment is a small crate or cage. For those who cringe at the thought of keeping a dog in a crate, you should keep in mind that it would be absolute insanity to leave an Italian Greyhound puppy alone in your home for a day or even an hour. A crate with a small pillow or blanket inside is an excellent place for the Italian Greyhound to rest and relax when you're not at home. The crate is also a tremendous asset in housebreaking, which I'll discuss in detail later. As long as the Italian Greyhound can turn around easily and lie down comfortably in the crate, he will feel a sense of security.

YOUR PUPPY'S NEW HOME

Before actually collecting your puppy, it is better that you purchase the basic items you will need in advance of the pup's arrival date. This allows you more opportunity to shop around and ensure you have exactly what you want rather than having to buy lesser quality in a hurry.

It is always better to collect the puppy as early in the day as possible. In most instances this will mean that the puppy has a few hours with your family before it is time to retire for his first night's sleep away from his former home.

If the breeder is local, then you may not need any form of box to place the puppy in when you bring him home. A member of the family can hold the pup in his lap—duly protected by some towels just in case the

A puppy's energy is boundless. It's a good idea to keep him occupied with various activities, such as playing Frisbee™.

puppy becomes car sick! Be sure to advise the breeder at what time you hope to arrive for the puppy, as this will obviously influence the feeding of the pup that morning or afternoon. If you arrive early in the day, then they will likely only give the pup a light breakfast so as to reduce the risk of travel sickness.

If the trip will be of a few hours duration, you should take a travel crate with you. The crate will provide your pup with a safe place to lie down and rest during the trip. During the trip, the puppy will no doubt wish to relieve his bowels, so you will have to make a few stops. On a long journey you may need a rest yourself, and can take the opportunity to let the puppy get some fresh air. However, do not let the puppy walk where there may have been a lot of other dogs because he might pick up an infection. Also, if he relieves his bowels at such a time, do not just leave the feces where they were dropped. This is the height of irresponsibility. It has resulted in many public parks and other places actually banning dogs. You can purchase poop-scoops from your pet shop and should have them with you whenever you are taking the dog out where he might foul a public place.

Opposite: Like all puppies, Italian Greyhound pups are adorable and irresistible. However, they still need a firm hand in guiding them through the trials of growing up.

Your journey home should be made as quickly as possible. If it is a hot day, be sure the car interior is amply supplied with fresh air. It should never be too hot or too cold for the puppy. The pup must never be placed where he might be subject to a draft. If the journey requires an overnight stop at a motel, be aware that other guests will not appreciate a puppy crying half the night. You must regard the puppy as a baby and comfort him so he does not cry for long periods. The worst thing you can do is to shout at or smack him. This will mean your relationship is off to a really bad start. You wouldn't smack a baby, and your puppy is still very much just this.

ON ARRIVING HOME

By the time you arrive home the puppy may be very tired, in which case he should be taken to his sleeping area and allowed to rest. Children should not be allowed to interfere with the pup when he is sleeping. If the pup is not tired, he can be allowed to investigate his new home—but always under your close supervision. After a short look around, the puppy will no doubt appreciate a light meal and a drink of water. Do not overfeed him at his first meal because he will be in an excited state and more likely to be sick.

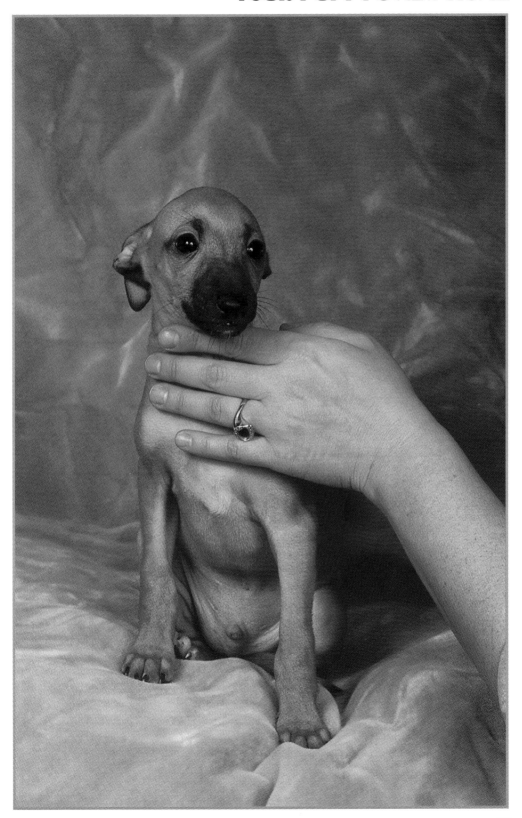

Although it is an obvious temptation, you should not invite friends and neighbors around to see the new arrival until he has had at least 48 hours in which to settle down. Indeed, if you can delay this longer then do so, especially if the puppy is not fully vaccinated. At the very least, the visitors might introduce some local bacteria on their clothing that the puppy is not immune to. This aspect is always a risk when a pup has been moved some distance, so the fewer people the pup meets in the first week or so the better.

DANGERS IN THE HOME

Your home holds many potential dangers for a little mischievous puppy, so you must think about these in advance and be sure he is protected from them. The more obvious are as follows:

Open Fires. All open fires should be protected by a mesh screen guard so there is no danger of the pup being burned by spitting pieces of coal or wood.

Electrical Wires. Puppies just love chewing on things, so be sure that all electrical appliances are neatly hidden from view and are not left plugged in when not in use. It is not sufficient simply to turn the plug switch to the off position—pull the plug from the socket.

Open Doors. A door would seem a pretty innocuous object, yet with a strong draft it could kill or injure a puppy easily if it is slammed shut. Always ensure there is no risk of this happening. It is most likely during warm weather when you have windows or outside doors open and a sudden gust of wind blows through.

Balconies. If you live in a high-rise building, obviously the pup must be protected from falling. Be sure he cannot get through any railings on your patio, balcony, or deck.

Ponds and Pools. A garden pond or a swimming pool is a very dangerous place for a little puppy to be near. Be sure it is well screened so there is no risk of the pup falling in. It takes barely a minute for a pup— or a child—to drown.

The Kitchen. While many puppies will be kept in the kitchen, at least while they are toddlers and not able to control their bowel movements, this is a room full of danger—especially while you are cooking. When cooking, keep the puppy in a play pen or in another room where he is safely out of harm's way. Alternatively, if you have a carry box or crate, put him

An Italian Greyhound's curiosity can get him into trouble. Keeping your dog behind a gate or in a crate is a good way to prevent accidents.

in this so he can still see you but is well protected.

Be aware, when using washing machines, that more than one puppy has clambered in and decided to have a nap and received a wash instead! If you leave the washing machine door open and leave the room for any reason, then be sure to check inside the machine before you close the door and switch on.

Small Children. Toddlers and small children should never be left unsupervised with puppies. In spite of such advice it is amazing just how many people not only do this but also allow children to pull and maul pups. They should be taught from the outset that a puppy is not a plaything to be dragged about the home—and they should be promptly scolded if they disobey.

Children must be shown how to lift a puppy so it is safe. Failure by you to correctly educate your children about dogs could one day result in their getting a very nasty bite or scratch. When a puppy is lifted, his weight must always be supported. To lift the pup, first place your right hand under his chest.

Next, secure the pup by using your left hand to hold his neck. Now you can lift him and bring him close to your chest. Never lift a pup by his ears and, while he can be lifted by the scruff of his neck where the fur is loose, there is no reason ever to do this, so don't.

Beyond the dangers already cited you may be able to think of other ones that are specific to your home—steep basement steps or the like. Go around your home and check out all potential problems—you'll be glad you did.

Puppies and children adore each other but be sure that you teach your child how to hold the puppy properly. If they are not careful, he can be injured.

THE FIRST NIGHT

The first few nights a puppy spends away from his mother and littermates are quite traumatic for him. He will feel very lonely, maybe cold, and will certainly miss the heartbeat of his siblings when sleeping. To help overcome his loneliness it may help to place a clock next to his bed—one with a loud tick. This will in some way soothe him, as the clock ticks to a rhythm not dissimilar from a heart beat. A cuddly toy may also help in the first few weeks. A dim nightlight may provide some comfort to the puppy, because his eyes will not yet be fully able to see in the dark. The puppy may want to leave his bed for a drink or to relieve himself.

If the pup does whimper in the night, there are two things you should not do. One is to get up and chastise him, because he will not understand why you are shouting at him; and the other is to rush to comfort him every time he cries because he will quickly realize that if he wants you to come running all he needs to do is to holler loud enough!

By all means give your puppy some extra attention on his first night, but after this quickly refrain from so doing. The pup will cry for a while but then settle down and go to sleep. Some pups are, of course, worse than others in this respect, so you must use balanced judgment in the matter. Many owners take their pups to bed with them, and there is certainly nothing wrong with this.

The pup will be no trouble in such cases. However, you should only do this if you intend to let this be a permanent arrangement, otherwise it is hardly fair to the puppy. If you have decided to have two puppies, then they will keep each other company and you will have few problems.

OTHER PETS

If you have other pets in the home then the puppy must be introduced to them under careful supervision. Puppies will get on just fine with any other pets—but you must make due allowance for the respective sizes of the pets concerned, and appreciate that your puppy has a rather playful nature. It would be very foolish to leave him with a young rabbit. The pup will want to play and might bite the bunny and get altogether too rough with it. Kittens are more able to defend themselves from overly cheeky pups, who will get a quick scratch if they overstep the mark. The

adult cat could obviously give the pup a very bad scratch, though generally cats will jump clear of pups and watch them from a suitable vantage point. Eventually they will meet at ground level where the cat will quickly hiss and box a puppy's ears. The pup will soon learn to respect an adult cat; thereafter they will probably develop into great friends as the pup matures into an adult dog.

Opposite: A puppy's first few nights in a new home can be frightening. Be as gentle and loving as possible to make your Italian Greyhound puppy feel safe and comfortable.

HOUSETRAINING

Undoubtedly, the first form of training your puppy will undergo is in respect to his toilet habits. To achieve this you can use either newspaper, or a large litter tray filled with soil or lined with newspaper. A puppy cannot control his bowels until he is a few months old, and not fully until he is an adult. Therefore you must anticipate his needs and be prepared for a few accidents. The prime times a pup will urinate and defecate are shortly after he wakes up from a sleep, shortly after he has eaten, and after he has been playing awhile. He will usually whimper and start searching the room for a suitable place. You must quickly pick him up and place him on the newspaper or in the litter tray. Hold him in position gently but firmly. He might jump out of the box without doing anything on the first one or two occasions, but if you simply repeat the procedure every time you think he wants to relieve himself then eventually he will get the message.

When he does defecate as required, give him plenty of praise, telling him what a good puppy he is. The litter tray or newspaper must, of course, be cleaned or replaced after each use—puppies do not like using a dirty toilet any more than you do. The pup's toilet can be placed near the kitchen door and as he gets older the tray can be placed outside while the door is open. The pup will then start to use it while he is outside. From that time on, it is easy to get the pup to use a given area of the yard.

Many breeders recommend the popular alternative of crate training. Upon bringing the pup home, introduce him to his crate. The open wire crate is the best choice, placed in a restricted, draft-free area of the home. Put the pup's Nylabone® and other favorite toys in the crate along with a wool blanket or other suitable bedding. The puppy's natural cleanliness instincts prohibit him from soiling in the place where he sleeps, his crate. The puppy should be allowed to

go in and out of the open crate during the day, but he should sleep in the crate at the night and at other intervals during the day. Whenever the pup is taken out of his crate, he should be brought outside (or to his newspapers) to do his business. Never use the crate as a place of punishment. You will see how quickly your pup takes to his crate, considering it as his own safe haven from the big world around him.

Crate training is an effective housetraining method for your Italian Greyhound puppy. Putting some of the puppy's favorite toys and food inside the crate makes it more appealing.

THE EARLY DAYS

You will no doubt be given much advice on how to bring up your puppy. This will come from dog-owning friends, neighbors, and through articles and books you may read on the subject. Some of the advice will be sound, some will be nothing short of rubbish. What you should do above all else is to keep an open mind and let common sense prevail over prejudice and worn-out ideas that have been handed down over the centuries. There is no one way that is superior to all others, no more than there is no one dog that is exactly a replica of another. Each is an individual and must always be regarded as such.

A dog never becomes disobedient, unruly, or a menace to society without the full consent of his owner. Your puppy may have many limitations, but the singular biggest limitation he is confronted with in so many instances is his owner's inability to understand his needs and how to cope with them.

IDENTIFICATION

It is a sad reflection on our society that the number of dogs and cats stolen every year runs into many thousands. To these can be added the number that get lost. If you do not want your cherished pet to be lost or stolen, then you should see that he is carrying a permanent identification number, as well as a temporary tag on his collar.

Permanent markings come in the form of tattoos placed either inside the pup's ear flap, or on the inner side of a pup's upper rear leg. The number given is then recorded with one of the national registration companies. Research laboratories will not purchase dogs carrying numbers as they realize these are clearly someone's pet, and not abandoned animals. As a result, thieves will normally abandon dogs so marked and this at least gives the dog a chance to be taken to the police or the dog pound, when the number can be traced and the dog reunited with its family. The only problem with this method at this time is that there are a number of registration bodies, so it is not always apparent which one the dog is registered with (as you provide the actual number). However, each registration body is aware of his competitors and will normally be happy to supply their addresses. Those holding the dog can check out which one you are with. It is not a perfect system, but until such is developed it's the best available.

A temporary tag takes the form of a metal or plastic disk large enough for you to place the dog's name and your phone number on it—maybe even your address as well. In virtually all places you will be required to obtain a license for your puppy. This may not become applicable until the pup is six months old, but it might apply regardless of his age. Much depends upon the state within a country, or the country itself, so check with your veterinarian if the breeder has not already advised you on this.

CARE OF YOUR ITALIAN GREYHOUND PUPPY

Anyone unfamiliar with the Italian Greyhound breed would never believe that the short, stubby, thick body of the Italian Greyhound puppy could develop into the slender, refined petite outline of the adult Greyhound. Like their cousins, the Whippets, Italian Greyhound puppies look nothing like adult Italian Greyhounds. To take it a step further, the Italian Greyhound puppy doesn't behave like the adult dog either. Although a true hound, the Italian Greyhound is still a Toy breed and needs to be treated like one, especially during the beginning stages of his life. The Italian Greyhound puppy is infantile and fragile, but at the same time, extremely busy and curious, which can be a dangerous combination. The Italian Greyhound puppy truly believes he is much larger than he really is.

Like most puppies, Italian Greyhounds are very curious and energetic. The first few days of life, however, your puppy will do little more than eat and sleep.

It's playtime for these Italian Greyhound pups. Keeping them occupied with bones and chew toys is a good method to prevent mischief.

I would like to re-emphasize the importance of preparing small children on how to safely handle and care for the young Italian Greyhound. Parental guidance is an essential part of the learning experience. Strongly discourage young children from picking the puppies up and carrying them around the house because the pups could be dropped unintentionally. Obviously, your child will be excited about the new dog's arrival and will want to participate in the raising and training of the dog. Take the time to show children how to properly lift a puppy—always supported by both hands, being gentle and cautious at all times.

If allowed to roam free, the curious, energetic Italian Greyhound puppy will often get himself into a position where he is vulnerable to possible injury. I've seen adult Italian Greyhounds get into places that one would think were virtually impossible for any animal to reach. For a hungry or curious Italian Greyhound, there is no place too high or out of reach. The worst mistake you can make is to yell or scold the dog when he's in such a jam. The Italian Greyhound will panic and leap into the air, almost certain to be injured. The proper way to remove your Italian Greyhound from such a predicament is

47

to slowly and calmly pick the dog up and place him on the ground. Despite all the hard work and training, you will occasionally find your Italian Greyhound doing something unpleasant. I once came out of my bedroom to find a female Italian Greyhound of mine munching a pepperoni pizza on the kitchen table.

For the Italian Greyhound, the transition from puppyhood to adolescence is much like a human being in his or her teenage years. Many changes take place in a developing Italian Greyhound. During the teething stage, Italian Greyhounds, like all Toy breeds in general, don't always lose all of their baby teeth on time. If this does occur and goes unnoticed, your Italian Greyhound may find himself with two sets of teeth that will collect unwanted food particles. If this condition is not taken care of, the dog could develop gum infections and other mouth problems. During the teething stage, you should provide various chew toys for your Italian Greyhound such as the Nylabone®, which will often do the trick in removing baby canines. If the baby teeth still don't fall out on their own, contact your veterinarian.

Despite all the safety precautions you can take in and out of your home, accidents unfortunately do happen. A topic that is frequently discussed among Italian Greyhound fanciers is leg breaking. Like I mentioned earlier, young Italian Greyhound puppies are curious and fearless, which will occasionally leave them perched on a high counter or some other undesirable place. If an Italian Greyhound is startled and takes a flying leap from such a spot, he may break a leg. In my opinion, leg breaking is an exaggerated issue that rarely occurs as long as you take the necessary precautions. My Italian Greyhounds run swiftly, leap great distances, and jump up to places that may not seem safe. The main difference is that my dogs are exercised everyday and aren't often crated. Italian Greyhounds that are left in a crate too long without a sufficient amount of exercise develop weak muscle structure and are more prone to break a leg when taking a leap from a high porch or table. An Italian Greyhound that is well exercised, properly fed, and trained will have a slim chance of ever breaking a leg. A further precaution in keeping the busy little Italian Greyhound on all four feet is to keep any enticing objects out of his reach, far enough so that temptation cannot get the best of him.

Opposite: Chow time for puppies is definitely one of their favorite parts of the day. Providing your puppy with the proper nutrition aids in good health and prevents illnesses.

FEEDING AND NUTRITION

THE ITALIAN GREYHOUND PUPPY AND ADULT

I cannot emphasize enough the importance of feeding your Italian Greyhound a balanced nutritional diet. With all of the many fine selections of dog foods in today's pet market, it's not at all difficult to feed your dog properly. Implementing good nutrition from the beginning helps the Italian Greyhound to develop both physically and mentally. Unfortunately, most nutritional mistakes stem from basic human nature. People enjoy the act of eating, and therefore try to pass that joy along to their dogs by offering them too many unhealthy treats.

The first step toward good nutrition is to ask the breeder about your new Italian Greyhound puppy's previous eating habits. If you plan to feed the puppy what he is used to eating, that's perfectly fine. If you choose to deviate from the original diet, make sure the change is made gradually. In most situations, the breeder will give you a minimum three-day supply of food to get you started.

If you gradually mix one or two tablespoons of the new food with the old, the transition is much easier for the puppy. An Italian Greyhound puppy will thrive on most quality commercial dog foods. Reputable dog foods that contain the proper amounts of vitamins and minerals help maintain the overall health of the Italian Greyhound. I strongly discourage Italian Greyhound owners from choosing homemade dog food diets because these tend to lack nutritional value. In their early stages, Italian Greyhound puppies must be fed small quantities of food at frequent intervals during an entire day. As the Italian Greyhound matures, the number of feedings should gradually decrease. An 8- to 10-

week-old Italian Greyhound should be kept at a good weight. He should be neither overweight nor underweight, but nice and smooth and properly proportioned. Physical appearance is an accurate indication of whether or not you are feeding your dog the correct amount.

HOW MUCH TO FEED AND WHEN

As a new Italian Greyhound owner, you will quickly learn that your little canine companions are ravenous eaters—their eyes are always bigger than their stomachs. Special precautions must be taken to prevent your Italian Greyhound from

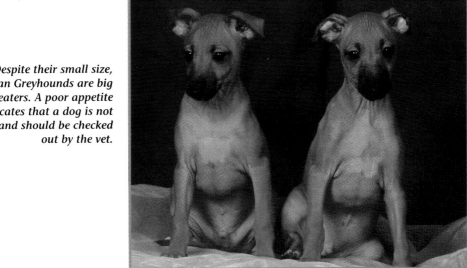

Despite their small size, Italian Greyhounds are big eaters. A poor appetite indicates that a dog is not well and should be checked out by the vet.

overeating and becoming obese. An Italian Greyhound with a poor appetite is a rarity and often signifies that the dog is not well. The key to implementing good eating habits begins with establishing a proper eating routine as a young puppy. As the Italian Greyhound matures, the amount of feeding intervals decreases. I prefer to feed one main meal that consists of approximately one cup of high-quality dry food, mixed with a little warm water and a small amount of canned food. In most circumstances, this is adequate for adult Italian Greyhounds. For puppies, I suggest providing them with one main meal, along with several smaller meals during the day. You must also take into consideration that not all Italian Greyhounds eat the same amount. The age of the dog and the amount of exercise he gets will also determine how much to feed him. Because food amounts differ from one dog to the next, you may need to increase or decrease the portions depending on the dog's weight. A good way to determine if your Italian Greyhound is at a correct weight is to feel around the stomach of the dog. If you can gently feel the ribs without too much excess skin, your Italian Greyhound is probably at a good weight. A well-conditioned Italian Greyhound should be muscular with just enough weight to present a smooth-flowing outline. If you feed your Italian Greyhound at a certain time every day, you should try to be consistent with the feedings. Some Italian Greyhound owners that are not home during the day will keep a small bowl of dry food that's readily accessible to the dogs. This is especially good for Italian Greyhound puppies that need to eat several times a day.

Opposite: Food plays a large role in a puppy's development. Make sure that you know not only the right food to feed your Italian Greyhound puppy, but the proper way to feed him as well.

THE ITALIAN GREYHOUND AND TABLE SCRAPS

The Italian Greyhound will eagerly accept and devour just about any type of food offered. There is nothing wrong with feeding your dog an occasional treat, provided it does not upset his basic diet. My Italian Greyhounds love all types of vegetables, such as peas, corn, green beans, celery, and lima beans. They are also very fond of potato chips, pretzels, pizza, cereal, bagels, oranges, and all types of pastas. Keep in mind that an excessive amount of junk food or table scraps can be harmful to your Italian Greyhound and as a general rule of thumb, foods that are bad for us are usually bad for our dogs. Although it is best to feed your dog high-quality commercial dog foods, table scraps are a fun alternative to the routine feeding schedule as long as they are kept minimal. Like humans, dogs can become obese, which is a condition detrimental to the health of the Italian Greyhound.

HOW TO FEED

How to feed your Italian Greyhound properly is as important as knowing what you should be feeding him. When feeding more than one dog, establishing good feeding patterns can make things easier. It's important to be consistent and remain on a fixed schedule, regardless of the number of times a day you feed your dog. If you're feeding more than one dog,

make sure to separate each bowl and dog, giving them their own private eating space. Some dogs tend to be bullies and will have no qualms about stealing the meals of their kennel mates. Try to get into the habit of never leaving food out for more than a few minutes. Your Italian Greyhound will learn to eat his meals quickly and sufficiently without dragging his bowl of food from one end of the house to the other, thinking it's playtime.

If you're using a combination of moist canned food and dry food, remember to refrigerate any unused portions to prevent spoilage. If your Italian Greyhound does not eat his entire meal, take it away and offer it again later on. Uneaten food that is allowed to sit for any length of time should be discarded. Remember to thoroughly wash the dog's bowl with warm water and soap after each feeding time. It is also extremely important to provide clean, fresh water at all times, especially during feeding. There are several different types and sizes of dog food bowls available. As long as your Italian Greyhound can eat comfortably from the bowl, you should have little difficulty. Just be sure to avoid a bowl that is obviously too large. I prefer weighted stainless steel bowls that fit neatly into holders and will often discourage rambunctious Italian Greyhound puppies from dumping out their dinner.

Stainless steel bowls such as this one are a good choice for feeding your Italian Greyhound. It's important to thoroughly wash the dog's bowls with warm water and soap after every meal to prevent bacteria from forming.

LIVING WITH YOUR ITALIAN GREYHOUND

The Italian Greyhound, like the Whippet and Greyhound, are one of the easiest breeds to groom. Like most short-coated dogs, the Italian Greyhound does not require much time for grooming. Although the Italian Greyhound will shed, the amount will be minimal if the coat is kept in good condition. The grooming tools and supplies required to keep your Italian Greyhound clean, trim, and neat are easily obtainable.

The grooming table is one of the most important tools in the grooming process. It becomes a safe place to cut your dog's nails and whiskers, brush his

Because of his short coat, the Italian Greyhound does not require extensive grooming. Keeping his coat in good condition will help lessen the amount of shedding.

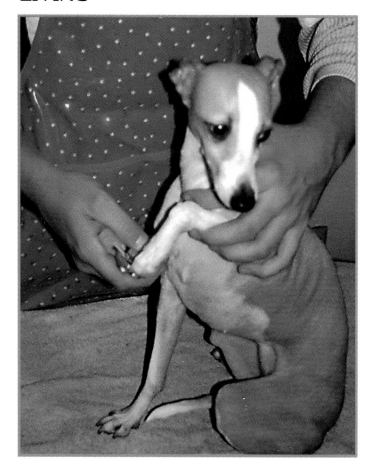

Nail clipping is an important part of your Italian Greyhound's grooming process. If his nails are not cut on a regular basis, he could develop foot injuries.

teeth, and clean his ears. Many show enthusiasts can use the table both indoors and outdoors as a convenient place to prepare their dogs for the show ring. Whether you're preparing your dog for a show, an obedience trial, or for company, a thorough grooming always starts with brushing. A regular soft brush or a gentle rubdown with your fingers will do the trick in removing loose, dead skin and hair. The Italian Greyhounds seem to really enjoy the brushing and it lends a lustrous shine to their coats as well.

BATHING AND NAIL CLIPPING

One of the most important parts of the grooming process is nail clipping. If your dog's nails are not cut on a regular basis (about every two or three weeks) your Italian Greyhound could suffer serious foot damage. Although every dog is different, your Italian Greyhound may not enjoy the nail clipping process. The key to having your Italian Greyhound stand still during this important procedure is to start the nail clipping at an early age. Even as young as two to three weeks of age, the Italian Greyhound should be getting used to nail clipping. Also, do not allow any bad behavior such as biting, shaking, or squirming. Begin by placing the puppy on a sturdy grooming table, giving him positive encouragement to stand. Place the Italian Greyhound under one arm while holding each foot securely and clip. Basically, there are two types of nail trimmers available. The regular hand-held nail clippers will do the job and there are several types to choose from. Many come with an adjustable guard to avoid cutting too much off the nail. The other type is an electric grinder that shortens the nails while buffing them at the same time. The grinder does an excellent job if you can get your Italian Greyhound comfortable with the grinding, buzzing sound.

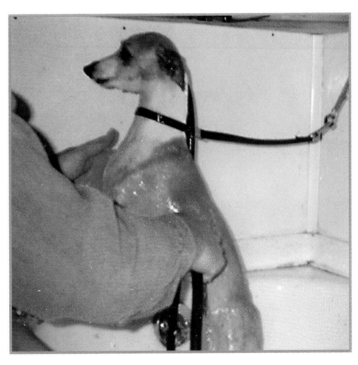

Some Italian Greyhounds love bathtime, while others will attempt to flee as quickly as possible. Using a leash during bath time can greatly reduce the risk of your Italian Greyhound jumping out and injuring himself.

When cutting your Italian Greyhound's nails, it is essential to have good lighting. You want to trim as closely to the quick as possible. The pink area inside the nail is the quick and if you cut into it, the dog's nail will bleed. If you do happen to cut the dog's nail too closely and the quick begins to bleed, apply some styptic product or cornstarch to stop the bleeding. If you feel uncomfortable cutting nails, contact a reliable dog groomer or breeder who will be able to cut them for you or at least assist you during the cutting. Like nail clipping, the secret to having an Italian Greyhound behave during his bath is to start when the dog is a young puppy. Some Italian Greyhounds will love the bathing experience while others will attempt to fly out of the bathtub like a rocket. The use of a leash suspended from above should keep the Italian Greyhound safely in place, greatly reducing the risk of the dog jumping out of the tub and injuring himself. The bathing water should be lukewarm and gently poured over the Italian Greyhound. Depending on the situation, you may use a mild, medicated, scented, or flea-and-tick shampoo. For best results, be sure to let the dog sit for 5-10 minutes before rinsing the lather away.

When cleaning your Italian Greyhound's ears, be very gentle as not to cause any damage.

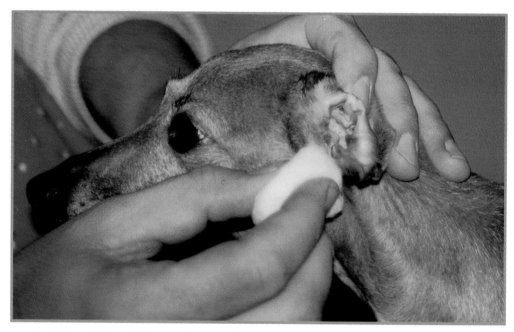

Unfortunately, all dogs will get fleas at sometime during their lives. An advantage of the Italian Greyhound's short hair is that it makes it easier to check for fleas or ticks; a fine flea comb will run smoothly through the Italian Greyhound's hair. Don't be alarmed if you do find some fleas or ticks on your Italian Greyhound. You can begin by treating your yard with flea and tick sprays. The next step is to spray the inside of your home or kennel, and around the sleeping quarters of the dog. The final step would be treating the dog himself. Make sure to use all-natural flea products on the Italian Greyhound. Strong flea sprays and shampoos can be extremely dangerous and possibly fatal to the Italian Greyhound. If you have any questions regarding flea sprays or shampoos, make sure you contact your local veterinarian before starting any flea and tick control program.

EARS, TEETH, AND WHISKERS

Cleaning the Italian Greyhound's ears is very simple. You may use a cotton swab, or preferably, a small cotton ball. Dip the cotton ball in some alcohol and squeeze out the excess liquid. Gently fold over the ear of the dog and carefully sweep the inside. Do not dig deeply into the ear or you may injure the dog. The purpose of ear cleaning is to take away any dirt or excess wax that might be built up on or around the ear canal. Frequent ear cleanings can help reduce ear infections and other ear-related problems.

A physical deficiency with the Italian Greyhound and Toy breeds in general is the teeth. Although the reason is somewhat uncertain, these small dogs require special dental attention. You will quickly realize that the tartar tends to build rapidly around the gums, leaving food particles to gather in between the teeth. If the tartar is not removed frequently, there will be early teeth loss. Tartar build-up will also lead to unpleasant dog breath, which will make you a little more hesitant when your Italian Greyhound tries to give you that next big, wet kiss.

Brushing your Italian Greyhound's teeth is a regular grooming necessity and probably one of the most unpleasant experiences for both you and the dog.

Although the reasons are uncertain, Italian Greyhounds require special dental attention. If you begin brushing your dog's teeth at an early age, he will become used to the process.

Most, if not all, Italian Greyhounds dislike having their teeth brushed. Again, starting the teeth cleaning procedure in the early puppy months is the best solution to having a cooperative Italian Greyhound. There are special dog toothbrushes available, along with dog toothpaste. I've found regular peroxide useful in getting their teeth very clean. The best way to remove tartar buildup is to use a dental pick. Unless you're an experienced breeder or veterinarian, tartar removal can be a complex procedure. For the safety of both you and your Italian Greyhound, I would recommend that only an experienced individual perform tartar removal. Although dog bones and dog chew toys help keep teeth somewhat clean, it can never replace a good weekly brushing or scaling.

Although it's not necessary, the trimming of the Italian Greyhound's whiskers will enhance the smooth outline of the head. If you intend to actively show your

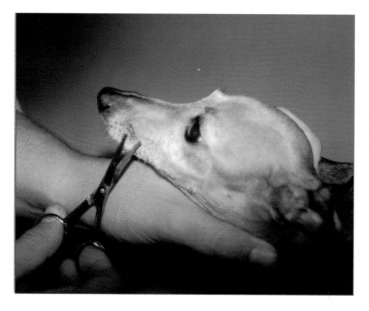

Trimming your Italian Greyhound's whiskers gives him a neat and clean appearance.

Italian Greyhound, the whiskers should be cut before each show. A small pair of blunt curved grooming scissors is the easiest tool to use. Most dogs are far more cooperative when it comes to whisker trimming than nail clipping or teeth brushing. These small blunt scissors will not cut the dog severely if he were to suddenly jerk away. Although whisker removal is optional in the show ring, I believe it gives the Italian Greyhound a far neater appearance than having a mouse-like face full of whiskers. Despite the belief of some dog fanciers that whisker removal is painful, the truth is just the opposite. Whisker removal causes the dog no pain and the dog has no use for them.

Some Italian Greyhound owners choose to trim other areas of the dog, such as the tail, neck, and ears for a cleaner and neater appearance. In addition, show exhibitors will apply coat spray to create a glossy, smooth, and silky coat, and many exhibitors use chalk to whiten parts of the dog's coat.

EXERCISE

The Italian Greyhound will undoubtedly live a healthier and happier life if provided with adequate space to exercise. The Italian Greyhound loves to run and play in a yard or field. Don't let their small size fool you—Italian Greyhounds are brisk runners and even better coursers. It's not at all uncommon for an Italian Greyhound to search out mice, squirrels, or even groundhogs if allowed to roam free over open acreage. Although a large fenced-in yard can be an ideal space for your Italian Greyhound to exercise, it's not necessary. Those who live in a city or a small apartment or condominium can still properly exercise their dogs. Taking your Italian Greyhound on a few

Italian Greyhounds are known to interact well with one another. These Italian Greyhounds play a fun game of ring-around-the-rosy.

The Italian Greyhound loves to be outside, as long as the weather is agreeable. This guy enjoys a perfect sunny day outdoors.

brisk walks every day will suffice. The walks will not only keep your Italian Greyhound healthy and fit, but also help socialize him at the same time. Retractable leads are popular and allow your Italian Greyhound to walk several feet in front of you without the restraint of a shorter leash. Not only will your Italian Greyhound learn how to behave while on a leash, he'll experience the different behaviors of other people and dogs. Furthermore, exercise will keep the Italian Greyhound mentally sound and help him overcome boredom, which commonly occurs with dogs that are left at home alone for long periods. Like humans, dogs also get depressed and need to relieve stress and tension. It's important to set aside a special playtime everyday for your Italian Greyhound.

There is nothing better than taking your Italian Greyhound on a trip to the park, camping, or on a daylong fishing trip. It doesn't take much time at all to teach your Italian Greyhound to run and retrieve a ball or small play toy. Keep in mind that the ball or toy should not be so small that the Italian Greyhound may swallow it or choke on it while at play. Italian Greyhounds that are given adequate exercise will develop strong muscles and overall body strength. At the same time, it's important to never overwork your Italian Greyhound when the weather is hot and humid. Exercise during these summer afternoons should be kept to a minimum. Italian Greyhounds love the warmth of the hot sun and will sunbathe for hours if allowed. Unfortunately, sunburn can become a serious problem and extra precaution should be taken to avoid having a baked Italian Greyhound. At the same time, the Italian Greyhound should not be overworked or exercised during very frigid winter days. The short coat of the Italian Greyhound will not keep him from withstanding severely cold temperatures, and the Italian Greyhound should not be left out during brutal winter days. I strongly recommend putting your Italian Greyhound outside whenever possible, as long as the weather cooperates. I keep my Italian Greyhounds outside for at least a brief period all year round, bringing them indoors during the evening, in a rainstorm, or when the temperature drops below freezing.

ACCOMMODATIONS

As mentioned in the previous section, the Italian Greyhound is not a breed that can withstand the rigors of outdoor living. Although the Italian Greyhound can adapt to a number of different environments, the severe cold is not one of them. The Italian Greyhound is a very durable animal and can withstand most winter days outside as long as the temperature doesn't drop below freezing for an extended length of time. Providing your Italian Greyhound with a sweater or coat can help him withstand the cold weather. Regardless of the time of year, the Italian Greyhound should be kept indoors during the evening. If you don't plan to bring the Italian Greyhound inside your home, you should at least provide a heated basement or kennel building. A small dog bed is very popular and will certainly be appreciated by your Italian Greyhound. A dog bed may be placed inside of your home or any specially designated area you have set up for your Italian Greyhound, preferably a warm, dry location. Unfortunately, some dogs have been known to chew apart their beds. If this does occur, perhaps a few chew toys will discourage such destructive be-

An exercise pen will help keep your Italian Greyhound safely confined while outdoors. These dogs wait their turn at a dog show.

havior. Most pet beds come with removable covers that may be easily washed and dried.

THE CRATE

The dog crate is probably one of the most important pieces of dog equipment that you will purchase. The crate should not be thought of as a cruel means of confinement, but as a safe area for your dog to rest and sleep while you are not at home. Besides, giving free reign of the house to an Italian Greyhound puppy when you are not at home could spell the instant destruction of your house. Anyone who has made the mistake of leaving a young Italian Greyhound unattended for more than five minutes should understand this. A crate is also a convenient place to keep your dog when houseguests are over or during mealtime. Many wire crates are even collapsible so that they may be easily folded, stored, and transported. The crate can also serve as a bed, provided you place comfortable bedding material in the exterior.

At first, don't be surprised if your Italian Greyhound doesn't readily accept the crate. The dog may whine or cry in the beginning during the initial adjustment period. If you want to make the crate more enticing, try placing some dog toys, treats, or your dog's bed inside the crate. Try locking your Italian Greyhound in the crate for short intervals, and then gradually increase the time he spends in the crate. In just a short time, your Italian Greyhound will learn to accept and enjoy the crate. He will learn to go in and out without any fuss, and will likely appreciate the privacy of having a comfortable place to call his own. The crate should be large enough so that your Italian Greyhound can stand up and move around comfortably. Although the crate is an excellent means of confinement, it should not be abused. Don't leave the Italian Greyhound in the crate for more than 8 to 10 hours and preferably less if possible. Excessive crating is not good for the dog's health and development.

INDOOR/OUTDOOR KENNEL RUNS

The indoor/outdoor kennel run is usually attached to a kennel building and makes for an excellent housing facility for the Italian Greyhound. Depending on the dog's preference, the kennel run allows your Italian Greyhound to have access to both the warmth and safety on the inside, and the sunshine and fresh air of the outdoors. A small doggy door allows him the freedom to come in and out very easily. A fenced-in run gives your Italian Greyhound plenty of outside exercise while you are at work and allows the dog to relieve himself if need be. If the weather turns poor, the Italian Greyhound can retreat inside without any difficulty. The kennel run is one of the most popular means of accommodating many different types of dog breeds and probably one of the safest.

Don't be surprised if your Italian Greyhound is most comfortable in your bed. Although many dog owners differ in opinion when it comes to allowing pets in their beds, the Italian Greyhound will not hesitate to jump into yours for some warmth and rest. In most circumstances, just sitting on your bed won't suffice, as the Italian Greyhound will insist on sleeping underneath the bed sheets no matter what the room temperature. On warm nights, your Italian Greyhound will remain hidden in the sheets and blankets until he reaches near heat exhaustion. Most of the time, I will usually drag mine out from underneath the layer of blankets so that they can breathe. Nothing will make your Italian Greyhound happier than letting him spend a night sleeping or grabbing an afternoon nap in bed with his cherished owners.

TRAINING YOUR ITALIAN GREYHOUND

Once your puppy has settled into your home and responds to his name, then you can begin his basic training. Before giving advice on how you should go about doing this, two important points should be made. You should train the puppy in isolation of any potential distractions, and you should keep all lessons very short. It is essential that you have the full attention of your puppy. This is not possible if there are other people about, or televisions and radios on, or other pets in the vicinity. Even when the pup has become a young adult, the maximum time you should allocate to a lesson is about 20 minutes. However,

All Italian Greyhound owners want a perfectly behaved puppy, but that takes effort. Patience, consistency, and firmness are the keys to successful training.

you can give the puppy more than one lesson a day, three being as many as are recommended, each well spaced apart.

Before beginning a lesson, always play a little game with the puppy so he is in an active state of mind and thus more receptive to the matter at hand. Likewise, always end a lesson with fun-time for the pup, and always—this is most important—end on a high note, praising the puppy. Let the lesson end when the pup has done as you require so he receives lots of fuss. This will really build his confidence.

Training your Italian Greyhound to a leash or collar is not as difficult as you might think. After the initial biting of the collar, the puppy will soon forget he even has one on.

COLLAR AND LEASH TRAINING

Training a puppy to his collar and leash is very easy. Place a collar on the puppy and, although he will initially try to bite at it, he will soon forget it, the more so if you play with him. You can leave the collar on for a few hours. Some people leave their dogs' collars on all of the time, others only when they are taking the dog out. If it is to be left on, purchase a narrow or round one so it does not mark the fur.

Once the puppy ignores his collar, then you can attach the leash to it and let the puppy pull this along behind it for a few minutes. However, if the pup starts to chew at the leash, simply hold the leash but keep it slack and let the pup go where he wants. The idea is to let him get the feel of the leash, but not get in the habit of chewing it. Repeat this a couple of times a day for two days and the pup will get used to the leash without thinking that it will restrain him—which you will not have attempted to do yet.

Next, you can let the pup understand that the leash will restrict his movements. The first time he realizes this, he will pull and buck or just sit down. Immediately call the pup to you and give him lots of fuss. Never tug on the leash so the puppy is dragged along the floor, as this simply implants a negative thought in his mind.

Basic training should begin as soon as the puppy arrives in your home. This Italian Greyhound stands poised and obedient.

THE COME COMMAND

Come is the most vital of all commands and especially so for the independently minded dog. To teach the puppy to come, let him reach the end of a long lead, then give the command and his name, gently pulling him toward you at the same time. As soon as he associates the word come with the action of moving toward you, pull only when he does not respond immediately. As he starts to come, move back to make him learn that he must come from a distance as well as when he is close to you. Soon you may be able to practice without a leash, but if he is slow to come or notably disobedient, go to him and pull him toward you, repeating the command. Never scold a dog during this exercise—or any other exercise. Remember the trick is that the puppy must want to come to you. For the very independent dog, hand signals may work better than verbal commands.

Italian Greyhounds are known for their jumping ability. Basic training will teach them when it is appropriate.

"Sit" "Down" and "Stay" are just some of the commands your Italian Greyhound should recognize. The author and his Italian Greyhound begin their basic training.

THE SIT COMMAND

As with most basic commands, your puppy will learn this one in just a few lessons. You can give the puppy two lessons a day on the sit command but he will make just as much progress with one 15-minute lesson each day. Some trainers will advise you that you should not proceed to other commands until the previous one has been learned really well. However, a bright young pup is quite capable of handling more than one command per lesson, and certainly per day. Indeed, as time progresses, you will be going through each command as a matter of routine before a new one is attempted. This is so the puppy always starts, as well as ends, a lesson on a high note, having successfully completed something.

Call the puppy to you and fuss over him. Place one hand on his hindquarters and the other under his upper chest. Say "Sit" in a pleasant (never harsh) voice. At the same time, push down his rear end and push up under his chest. Now lavish praise on the puppy. Repeat this a few times and your pet will get the idea. Once the puppy is in the sit position you will release your hands. At first he will tend to get up, so immediately repeat the exercise. The lesson will end when the pup is in the sit position. When the puppy understands the command, and does it right away, you can slowly move backwards so that you are a few feet away from him. If he attempts to come to you, simply place him back in the original position and start again. Do not attempt to keep the pup in the sit position for too long. At this age, even a few seconds is a long while and you do not want him to get bored with lessons before he has even begun them.

THE HEEL COMMAND

All dogs should be able to walk nicely on a leash without their owners being involved in a tug-of-war. The heel command will follow leash training. Heel training is best done where you have a wall to one side of you. This will restrict the puppy's lateral movements, so you only have to contend with forward and backward situations. A fence is an alternative, or you can do the lesson in the garage. Again, it is better to do the lesson in private, not on a public sidewalk where there will be many distractions.

Bred for companionship, the Italian Greyhound gets along great with people of all ages. This cute Italian Greyhound gets hugs and kisses from a good friend.

71

With a puppy, there will be no need to use a choke collar as you can be just as effective with a regular one. The leash should be of good length, certainly not too short. You can adjust the space between you, the puppy, and the wall so your pet has only a small amount of room to move sideways. This being so, he will either hang back or pull ahead—the latter is the more desirable state as it indicates a bold pup who is not frightened of you.

Hold the leash in your right hand and pass it through your left. As the puppy moves ahead and strains on the leash, give the leash a quick jerk backwards with your left hand, at the same time saying "Heel." The position you want the pup to be in is such that his chest is level with, or just behind,

An obedience-trained dog will listen when his owner commands him. This Italian Greyhound learns how to heel properly.

an imaginary line from your knee. When the puppy is in this position, praise him and begin walking again, and the whole exercise will be repeated. Once the puppy begins to get the message, you can use your left hand to pat the side of your knee so the pup is encouraged to keep close to your side.

It is useful to suddenly do an about-turn when the pup understands the basics. The puppy will now be behind you, so you can pat your knee and say "Heel." As soon as the pup is in the correct position, give him lots of praise. The puppy will now be beginning to associate certain words with certain actions. Whenever he is not in the heel position he will experience displeasure as you jerk the leash, but when he comes alongside you he will receive praise. Given these two options, he will always prefer the latter—assuming he has no other reason to fear you, which would then create a dilemma in his mind.

Once the lesson has been well learned, then you can adjust your pace from a slow walk to a quick one and the puppy will come to adjust. The slow walk is always the more difficult for most puppies, as they are usually anxious to be on the move.

If you have no wall to walk against then things will be a little more difficult because the pup will tend to wander to his left. This means you need to give lateral jerks as well as bring the pup to your side. End the lesson when the pup is walking nicely beside you. Begin the lesson with a few sit commands (which he understands by now), so you're starting with success and praise. If your puppy is nervous on the leash, you should never drag him to your side as you may see so many other people do (who obviously didn't invest in a good book like you did!). If the pup sits down, call him to your side and give lots of praise. The pup must always come to you because he wants to. If he is dragged to your side he will see you doing the dragging—a big negative. When he races ahead he does not see you jerk the leash, so all he knows is that something restricted his movement and, once he was in a given position, you gave him lots of praise. This is using canine psychology to your advantage.

Always try to remember that if a dog must be disciplined, then try not to let him associate the discipline with you. This is not possible in all matters but, where it is, this is definitely to be preferred.

A dog that behaves in the proper manner is a pleasure to be around. This mommy-to-be looks perfectly content standing exactly where she is.

THE STAY COMMAND

This command follows from the sit. Face the puppy and say "Sit." Now step backwards, and as you do, say "Stay." Let the pup remain in the position for only a few seconds before calling him to you and giving lots of praise. Repeat this, but step further back. You do not need to shout at the puppy. Your pet is not deaf; in fact, his hearing is far better than yours. Speak just loudly enough for the pup to hear, yet use a firm voice. You can stretch the word to form a "sta-a-a-y." If the pup gets up and comes to you simply lift him up, place him back in the original position, and start again. As the pup comes to understand the command, you can move further and further back.

The next test is to walk away after placing the pup. This will mean your back is to him, which will tempt him to follow you. Keep an eye over your shoulder, and the minute the pup starts to move, spin around and, using a sterner voice, say either "Sit" or "Stay." If the pup has gotten quite close to you, then, again, return him to the original position.

As the weeks go by you can increase the length of time the pup is left in the stay position—but two to three minutes is quite long enough for a puppy. If your puppy drops into a lying position and is clearly more comfortable, there is nothing wrong with this. Likewise, your pup will want to face the direction in which you walked off. Some trainers will insist that the dog faces the direction he was placed in, regardless of whether you move off on his blind side. I have never believed in this sort of obedience because it has no practical benefit.

THE DOWN COMMAND

From the puppy's viewpoint, the down command can be one of the more difficult ones to accept. This is because the position is one taken up by a submissive dog in a wild pack situation. A timid dog will roll over—a natural gesture of submission. A bolder pup will want to get up, and might back off, not feeling he should have to submit to this command. He will feel that he is under attack from you and about to be punished—which is what would be the position in his natural environment. Once he comes to understand this is not the case, he will accept this unnatural position without any problem.

You may notice that some dogs will sit very quickly, but will respond to the down command more slowly—it is their way of saying that they will obey the command, but under protest!

There two ways to teach this command. One is, in my mind, more intimidating than the other, but it is up

These two Italian Greyhounds demonstrate how to "stay" in a sitting position.

to you to decide which one works best for you. The first method is to stand in front of your puppy and bring him to the sit position, with his collar and leash on. Pass the leash under your left foot so that when you pull on it, the result is that the pup's neck is forced downwards. With your free left hand, push the pup's shoulders down while at the same time saying "Down." This is when a bold pup will instantly try to back off and wriggle in full protest. Hold the pup firmly by the shoulders so he stays in the position for a second or two, then tell him what a good dog he is and give him lots of praise. Repeat this only a few times in a lesson because otherwise the puppy will get bored and upset over this command. End with an easy command that brings back the pup's confidence.

The second method, and the one I prefer, is done as follows: Stand in front of the pup and then tell him to sit. Now kneel down, which is immediately far less intimidating to the puppy than to have you towering above him. Take each of his front legs and pull them forward, at the same time saying "Down." Release the legs and quickly apply light pressure on the shoulders with your left hand. Then, as quickly, say "Good boy" and give lots of fuss. Repeat two or three times only. The pup will learn over a few lessons. Remember, this is a very submissive act on the pup's behalf, so there is no need to rush matters.

RECALL TO HEEL COMMAND

When your puppy is coming to the heel position from an off-leash situation—such as if he has been running free—he should do this in the correct manner. He should pass behind you and take up his position and then sit. To teach this command, have the pup in front of you in the sit position with his collar and leash on. Hold the leash in your right hand. Give him the command to heel, and pat your left knee. As the pup starts to move forward, use your right hand to guide him behind you. If need be you can hold his collar and walk the dog around the back of you to the desired position. You will need to repeat this a few times until the dog understands what is wanted.

When he has done this a number of times, you can try it without the collar and leash. If the pup comes up toward your left side, then bring him to the sit position in front of you, hold his collar and walk him around the back of you. He will eventually understand and automatically pass around your back each time. If the dog

This well-behaved puppy has learned how to sit quietly and obey his master's commands.

is already behind you when you recall him, then he should automatically come to your left side, which you will be patting with your hand.

THE NO COMMAND

This is a command that must be obeyed every time without fail. There are no halfway stages, he must be 100-percent reliable. Most delinquent dogs have never been taught this command; included in these are the jumpers, the barkers, and the biters. Were your puppy to approach a poisonous snake or any other potential danger, the no command, coupled with the recall, could save his life. You do not need to give a specific lesson for this command because it will crop up time and again in day-to-day life.

If the puppy is chewing a slipper, you should approach the pup, take hold of the slipper, and say "No" in a stern voice. If he jumps onto the furniture, lift him off and say "No" and place him gently on the floor. You must be consistent in the use of the command and apply it every time he is doing something you do not want him to do.

YOUR HEALTHY ITALIAN GREYHOUND

Dogs, like all other animals, are capable of contracting problems and diseases that, in most cases, are easily avoided by sound husbandry—meaning well-bred and well-cared-for animals are less prone to developing diseases and problems than are carelessly bred and neglected animals. Your knowledge of how to avoid problems is far more valuable than all of the books and advice on how to cure them. Respectively, the only person you should listen to about treatment is your vet. Veterinarians don't have all the answers, but at least they are trained to analyze and treat illnesses, and are aware of the full implications of treatments. This does not mean a few old remedies aren't good standbys when all else fails, but in most cases modern science provides the best treatments for disease.

PHYSICAL EXAMS

Your puppy should receive regular physical examinations or check-ups. These come in two forms. One is obviously performed by your vet, and the other is a day-to-day procedure that should be done by you. Apart from the fact the exam will highlight any problem at an early stage, it is an excellent way of socializing the pup to being handled.

To do the physical exam yourself, start at the head and work your way around the body. You are looking for any sign of lesions, or any indication of parasites on the pup. The most common parasites are fleas and ticks.

Opposite: As a responsible Italian Greyhound owner, you should have an understanding of the medical problems that affect the breed.

Italian Greyhounds require special dental care for overall good health.

HEALTHY TEETH AND GUMS

Chewing is instinctual. Puppies chew so that their teeth and jaws grow strong and healthy as they develop. As the permanent teeth begin to emerge, it is painful and annoying to the puppy, and puppy owners must recognize that their new charges need something safe upon which to chew. Unfortunately, once the puppy's permanent teeth have emerged and settled solidly into the jaw, the chewing instinct does not fade. Adult dogs instinctively need to clean their teeth, massage their gums, and exercise their jaws through chewing.

It is necessary for your dog to have clean teeth. You should take your dog to the veterinarian at least once a year to have his teeth cleaned and to have his mouth examined for any sign of oral disease. Although dogs do not get cavities in the same way humans do, dogs'

The Hercules® by Nylabone® has raised dental tips that help fight plaque on your Italian Greyhound's teeth and gums.

teeth accumulate tartar, and more quickly than humans do! Veterinarians recommend brushing your dog's teeth daily. But who can find time to brush their dog's teeth daily? The accumulation of tartar and plaque on our dog's teeth when not removed can cause irritation and eventually erode the enamel and finally destroy the teeth. Advanced cases, while destroying the teeth, bring on gingivitis and periodontitis, two very serious conditions that can affect the dog's internal organs as well...to say nothing about bad breath!

Raised dental tips on the surface of every Plaque Attacker™ help to combat plaque and tartar.

Since everyone can't brush their dog's teeth daily or get to the veterinarian often enough for him to scale

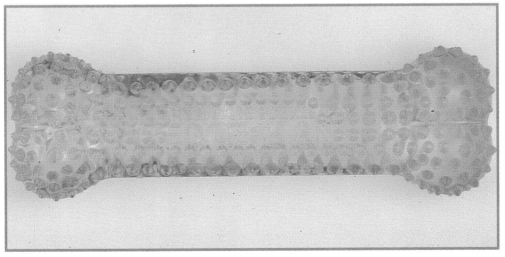

the dog's teeth, providing the dog with something safe to chew on will help maintain oral hygeine. Chew devices from Nylabone® keep dogs' teeth clean, but they also provide an excellent resource for entertainment and relief of doggie tensions. Nylabone® products give your dog something to do for an hour or two every day and during that hour or two, your dog will be taking an active part in keeping his teeth and gums healthy…without even realizing it! That's invaluable to your dog, and valuable to you!

Nylabone® provides fun bones, challenging bones, and *safe* bones. It is an owner's responsibility to recognize safe chew toys from dangerous ones. Your dog will chew and devour anything you give him. Dogs must not be permitted to chew on items that they can break. Pieces of broken objects can do internal damage to a dog, besides ripping the dog's mouth. Cheap plastic or rubber toys can cause stoppage in the intestines; such stoppages are operable only if caught immediately.

The most obvious choices, in this case, may be the worst choice. Natural beef bones were not designed for chewing and cannot take too much pressure from the sides. Due to the abrasive nature of these bones, they should be offered most sparingly. Knuckle bones, though once very popular for dogs, can be easily

Nylabone® is the only plastic dog bone made of 100% virgin nylon, specially processed to create a tough, durable, completely safe bone.

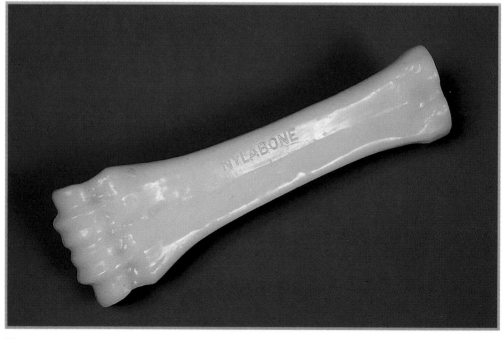

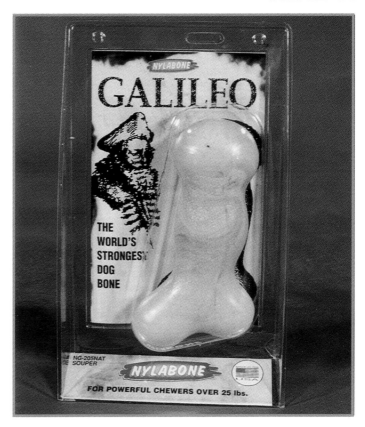

The Galileo™ is flavored to appeal to your dog and annealed so it has a relatively soft outer layer.

chewed up and eaten by dogs. At the very least, digestion is interrupted; at worst, the dog can choke or suffer from intestinal blockage.

When a dog chews hard on a Nylabone®, little bristle-like projections appear on the surface of the bone. These help to clean the dog's teeth and add to the gum-massaging. Given the chemistry of the nylon, the bristle can pass through the dog's intestinal tract without effect. Since nylon is inert, no microorganism can grow on it, and it can be washed in soap and water or sterilized in boiling water or in an autoclave.

For the sake of your dog, his teeth and your own peace of mind, provide your dog with Nylabones®. They have 100 variations from which to choose.

FIGHTING FLEAS

Fleas are very mobile and may be red, black, or brown in color. The adults suck the blood of the host, while the larvae feed on the feces of the adults, which is rich in blood. Flea "dirt" may be seen on the pup as very tiny clusters of blackish specks that look like freshly ground pepper. The eggs of fleas may be laid on the puppy, though they are more commonly laid off the host in a favorable place, such as the bedding. They normally hatch in 4 to 21 days, depending on the temperature, but they can survive for up to 18 months if temperature conditions are not favorable. The larvae are maggot-like and molt a couple of times before forming pupae, which can survive long periods until the temperature, or the vibration of a nearby host, causes them to emerge and jump on a host.

There are a number of effective treatments available, and you should discuss them with your veterinarian, then follow all instructions for the one you choose. Any treatment will involve a product for your puppy or dog and one for the environment, and will require diligence on your part to treat all areas and thoroughly clean your home and yard until the infestation is eradicated.

THE TROUBLE WITH TICKS

Ticks are arthropods of the spider family, which means they have eight legs (though the larvae have six). They bury their headparts into the host and gorge on its blood. They are easily seen as small grain-like creatures sticking out from the skin. They are often picked up when dogs play in fields, but may also arrive in your yard via wild animals—even birds—or stray cats and dogs. Some ticks are species-specific, others are more adaptable and will host on many species.

The cat flea is the most common flea of dogs. It starts feeding soon after it makes contact with the dog.

The deer tick is the most common carrier of Lyme disease. Photo courtesy of Virbac Laboratories, Inc., Fort Worth, Texas.

The most troublesome type of tick is the deer tick, which spreads the deadly Lyme disease that can cripple a dog (or a person). Deer ticks are tiny and very hard to detect. Often, by the time they're big enough to notice, they've been feeding on the dog for a few days—long enough to do their damage. Lyme disease was named for the area of the United States in which it was first detected—Lyme, Connecticut— but has now been diagnosed in almost all parts of the U.S. Your veterinarian can advise you of the danger to your dog(s) in your area, and may suggest your dog be vaccinated for Lyme. Always go over your dog with a fine-toothed flea comb when you come in from walking through any area that may harbor deer ticks, and if your dog is acting unusually sluggish or sore, seek veterinary advice.

Attempts to pull a tick free will invariably leave the headpart in the pup, where it will die and cause an infected wound or abscess. The best way to remove ticks is to dab a strong saline solution, iodine, or alcohol on them. This will numb them, causing them to loosen their hold, at which time they can be removed with forceps. The wound can then be cleaned and covered with an antiseptic ointment. If ticks are common in your area, consult with your vet for a suitable pesticide to be used in kennels, on bedding, and on the puppy or dog.

INSECTS AND OTHER OUTDOOR DANGERS

There are many biting insects, such as mosquitoes, that can cause discomfort to a puppy. Many diseases are transmitted by the males of these species.

A pup can easily get a grass seed or thorn lodged between his pads or in the folds of his ears. These may go unnoticed until an abscess forms.

This is where your daily check of the puppy or dog will do a world of good. If your puppy has been playing in long grass or places where there may be thorns, pine needles, wild animals, or parasites, the check-up is a wise precaution.

Parasites like fleas and ticks can affect your dog after playing outside. Be sure to check your Italian Greyhound's coat thoroughly when coming in from outdoors.

SKIN DISORDERS

Apart from problems associated with lesions created by biting pests, a puppy may fall foul to a number of other skin disorders. Examples are ringworm, mange, and eczema. Ringworm is not caused by a worm, but is a fungal infection. It manifests itself as a sore-looking bald circle. If your puppy should have any form of bald patches, let your veterinarian check him over; a microscopic examination can confirm the condition. Many old remedies for ringworm exist, such as iodine, carbolic acid, formalin, and other tinctures, but modern drugs are superior.

Fungal infections can be very difficult to treat, and even more difficult to eradicate, because of the spores. These can withstand most treatments, other than burning, which is the best thing to do with bedding once the condition has been confirmed.

Mange is a general term that can be applied to many skin conditions where the hair falls out and a flaky crust develops and falls away.

Often, dogs will scratch themselves, and this invariably is worse than the original condition, for it opens lesions that are then subject to viral, fungal, or parasitic attack. The cause of the problem can be various species of mites. These either live on skin debris and the hair follicles, which they destroy, or they bury themselves just beneath the skin and feed on the tissue. Applying general remedies from pet stores is not recommended because it is essential to identify the type of mange before a specific treatment is effective.

Eczema is another non-specific term applied to many skin disorders. The condition can be brought about in many ways. Sunburn, chemicals, allergies to foods, drugs, pollens, and even stress can all produce a deterioration of the skin and coat. Given the range of causal factors, treatment can be difficult because the problem is one of identification. It is a case of taking each possibility at a time and trying to correctly diagnose the matter. If the cause is of a dietary nature then you must remove one item at a time in order to find out if the dog is allergic to a given food. It could, of course, be the lack of a nutrient that is the problem, so if the condition persists, you should consult your veterinarian.

INTERNAL DISORDERS

It cannot be overstressed that it is very foolish to attempt to diagnose an internal disorder without the advice of a veterinarian. Take a relatively common problem such as diarrhea. It might be caused by nothing more serious than the puppy hogging a lot of food or eating something that it has never previously eaten. Conversely, it could be the first indication of a potentially fatal disease. It's up to your veterinarian to make the correct diagnosis.

The following symptoms, especially if they accompany each other or are progressively added to earlier symptoms, mean you should visit the veterinarian right away:

Continual vomiting. All dogs vomit from time to time and this is not necessarily a sign of illness. They will eat grass to induce vomiting. It is a natural cleansing process common to many carnivores. However, continued vomiting is a clear sign of a problem. It may be a blockage in the pup's intestinal tract, it may be induced by worms, or it could be due to any number of diseases.

Diarrhea. This, too, may be nothing more than a temporary condition due to many factors. Even a change of home can induce diarrhea, because this often stresses the pup, and invariably there is some change in the diet. If it persists more than 48 hours then something is amiss. If blood is seen in the feces, waste no time at all in taking the dog to the vet.

Running eyes and/or nose. A pup might have a chill and this will cause the eyes and nose to weep. Again, this should quickly clear up if the puppy is placed in a warm environment and away from any drafts. If it does not, and especially if a mucous discharge is seen, then the pup has an illness that must be diagnosed.

Coughing. Prolonged coughing is a sign of a problem, usually of a respiratory nature.

Wheezing. If the pup has difficulty breathing and makes a wheezing sound when breathing, then something is wrong.

Cries when attempting to defecate or urinate. This might only be a minor problem due to the hard state of the feces, but it could be more serious, especially if the pup cries when urinating.

Cries when touched. Obviously, if you do not handle a puppy with care he might yelp. However, if he cries even when lifted gently, then he has an internal problem that becomes apparent when pressure is applied to a given area of the body. Clearly, this must be diagnosed.

Refuses food. Generally, puppies and dogs are greedy creatures when it comes to feeding time. Some might be more fussy, but none should refuse more than one meal. If they go for a number of hours without showing any interest in their food, then something is not as it should be.

General listlessness. All puppies have their off days when they do not seem their usual cheeky, mischievous selves. If this condition persists for more than two days then there is little doubt of a problem. They may not show any of the signs listed, other than perhaps a reduced interest in their food. There are many diseases that can develop internally without displaying obvious clinical signs. Blood, fecal, and other tests are needed in order to identify the disorder before it reaches an advanced state that may not be treatable.

WORMS

There are many species of worms, and a number of these live in the tissues of dogs and most other animals. Many create no problem at all, so you are not even aware they exist. Others can be tolerated in small levels, but become a major problem if they number more than a few. The most common types seen in dogs are roundworms and tapeworms. While roundworms are the greater problem, tapeworms require an intermediate host so are more easily eradicated.

Roundworms are spaghetti-like worms that cause a pot-bellied appearance and dull coat, along with more severe symptoms, such as diarrhea and vomiting. Photo courtesy of Merck AgVet.

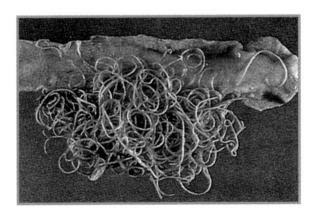

Roundworms of the species *Toxocara canis* infest the dog. They may grow to a length of 8 inches (20 cm) and look like strings of spaghetti. The worms feed on the digesting food in the pup's intestines. In chronic cases the puppy will become pot-bellied, have diarrhea, and will vomit. Eventually, he will stop eating, having passed through the stage when he always seems hungry. The worms lay eggs in the puppy and these pass out in his feces. They are then either ingested by the pup, or they are eaten by mice, rats, or beetles. These may then be eaten by the puppy and the life cycle is complete.

Larval worms can migrate to the womb of a pregnant bitch, or to her mammary glands, and this is how they pass to the puppy. The pregnant bitch can be wormed, which will help. The pups can, and should,

Whipworms are hard to find unless you strain your dog's feces, and this is best left to a veterinarian. Pictured here are adult whipworms.

be wormed when they are about two weeks old. Repeat worming every 10 to 14 days and the parasites should be removed. Worms can be extremely dangerous to young puppies, so you should be sure the pup is wormed as a matter of routine.

Tapeworms can be seen as tiny rice-like eggs sticking to the puppy's or dog's anus. They are less destructive, but still undesirable. The eggs are eaten by mice, fleas, rabbits, and other animals that serve as intermediate hosts. They develop into a larval stage and the host must be eaten by the dog in order to complete the chain. Your vet will supply a suitable remedy if tapeworms are seen or suspected. There are other worms, such as hookworms and whipworms, that are also blood suckers. They will make a pup anemic, and blood might be seen in the feces, which can be examined by the vet to confirm their presence. Cleanliness in all matters is the best preventative measure for all worms.

Heartworm infestation in dogs is passed by mosquitoes but can be prevented by a monthly (or daily) treatment that is given orally. Talk to your vet about the risk of heartworm in your area.

BLOAT (GASTRIC DILATATION)

This condition has proved fatal in many dogs, especially large and deep-chested breeds, such as the Weimaraner and the Great Dane. However, any dog can get bloat. It is caused by swallowing air during exercise, food/water gulping or another strenuous task. As many believe, it is not the result of flatulence. The stomach of an affected dog twists, disallowing food and blood flow and resulting in harmful toxins being released into the bloodstream. Death can easily follow if the condition goes undetected.

The best preventative measure is not to feed large meals or exercise your puppy or dog immediately after he has eaten. Veterinarians recommend feeding three smaller meals per day in an elevated feeding rack, adding water to dry food to prevent gulping, and not offering water during mealtimes.

VACCINATIONS

Every puppy, purebred or mixed breed, should be vaccinated against the major canine diseases. These are distemper, leptospirosis, hepatitis, and canine parvovirus. Your puppy may have received a temporary vaccination against distemper before you purchased him, but be sure to ask the breeder to be sure.

The age at which vaccinations are given can vary, but will usually be when the pup is 8 to 12 weeks old. By this time any protection given to the pup by antibodies received from his mother via her initial milk feeds will be losing their strength.

The puppy's immune system works on the basis that the white blood cells engulf and render harmless

Rely on your veterinarian for the most effectual vaccination schedule for your Italian Greyhound puppy.

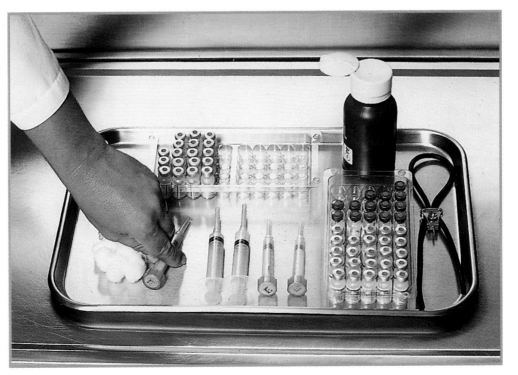

attacking bacteria. However, they must first recognize a potential enemy.

Vaccines are either dead bacteria or they are live, but in very small doses. Either type prompts the pup's defense system to attack them. When a large attack then comes (if it does), the immune system recognizes it and massive numbers of lymphocytes (white blood corpuscles) are mobilized to counter the attack. However, the ability of the cells to recognize these dangerous viruses can diminish over a period of time. It is therefore useful to provide annual reminders about the nature of the enemy. This is done by means of booster injections that keep the immune system on its alert. Immunization is not 100-percent guaranteed to be successful, but is very close. Certainly it is better than giving the puppy no protection.

Dogs are subject to other viral attacks, and if these are of a high-risk factor in your area, then your vet will suggest you have the puppy vaccinated against these as well.

Your puppy or dog should also be vaccinated against the deadly rabies virus. In fact, in many places it is illegal for your dog not to be vaccinated. This is to protect your dog, your family, and the rest of the animal population from this deadly virus that infects the nervous system and causes dementia and death.

ACCIDENTS

All puppies will get their share of bumps and bruises due to the rather energetic way they play. These will usually heal themselves over a few days. Small cuts should be bathed with a suitable disinfectant and then smeared with an antiseptic ointment. If a cut looks more serious, then stem the flow of blood with a towel or makeshift tourniquet and rush the pup to the veterinarian. Never apply so much pressure to the wound that it might restrict the flow of blood to the limb.

In the case of burns you should apply cold water or an ice pack to the surface. If the burn was due to a chemical, then this must be washed away with copious amounts of water. Apply petroleum jelly, or any vegetable oil, to the burn. Trim away the hair if need be. Wrap the dog in a blanket and rush him to the vet. The pup may go into shock, depending on the severity of the burn, and this will result in a lowered blood pressure, which is dangerous and the reason the pup must receive immediate veterinary attention.